Butterfly

Written by Stephen Savage

Illustrated by André Boos

Thomson Learning
New York

OBSERVING NATURE

Ant   Duck

Butterfly   Frog

First published in the
United States in 1995 by
Thomson Learning
115 Fifth Avenue
New York, NY 10003

First published in
Great Britain in 1994 by
Wayland (Publishers) Ltd.

Library of Congress Cataloging-in-
Publication Data
Savage, Stephen.
 Butterfly/ written by Stephen Savage;
illustrated by André Boos.
     p.   cm.—(Observing nature)
 Includes index.
 ISBN 1-56847-325-7
 1. Butterflies—Juvenile literature.
[1. Butterflies.] I. Boos, André. II. Title.
III. Series: Savage, Stephen, 1965-
Observing nature.
QL544.2.S36   1995
595.78'9—dc20   94-31290

Printed in Italy

Contents

What Is a Butterfly?

Butterflies are insects. There are many types. The wings of most butterflies are covered in beautiful, brightly colored patterns. These patterns are made of thousands of colored scales the size of dust.

Butterflies need to warm up each day before they can fly. They rest in the sunlight with their wings stretched out. Peacock butterflies, and many other kinds, can be seen in gardens, fields, and woodlands in different parts of the world.

Some people confuse butterflies and moths. Both change from caterpillar to pupa to adult. But butterflies and moths are different animals.

Butterfly or Moth?

Butterflies fly in the daytime and most moths fly at night. There are some types of moths that do fly in daylight. How do you know if you are looking at a butterfly or a moth?

Butterflies and moths are very similar, but if you look closely you will notice some differences. Most butterflies have long feelers on their heads with a small knob on the end. They often close their wings when resting, and most are brightly colored.

Most moths have hairlike
or feathery feelers, thicker
hairy bodies, and cannot
close their wings. Many
types are dark-
colored, but there
are some brightly
colored types.

Hibernation

The peacock butterfly, the mourning
cloak butterfly, and the anglewing
butterfly sleep in the cold winter
months. As the weather becomes
colder, they look for a safe place to
spend the winter. This may be in a
hollow tree or in a dark corner of a
shed. Once one of these butterflies
finds a safe place, it goes into a deep
sleep. Some even hang upside down.
It will not eat or move for six months.

Some other types of butterflies
hibernate in a shell-like chrysalis,
and some fly to warmer areas.

8

Mating

In the spring, flowers begin to grow in the warm sunshine. This is when hibernating butterflies awake. They feed on a sugary liquid, called nectar, made by flowers. When butterflies appear in your backyard, you'll know that spring is here at last.

In sunny weather, butterflies can be seen flying from flower to flower. After a few weeks, the male and female butterflies are ready to mate.

The Eggs

After mating, the female butterfly lays her eggs. Some types of butterflies lay their eggs on the underside of leaves. A few other types simply scatter their eggs as they fly. Most butterflies will lay hundreds of eggs because many will be eaten by other animals.

12

Each egg is protected by a thin shell.
The baby caterpillars grow inside
the eggs until they are ready
to hatch. They feed on a
special food inside the
egg called yolk. If the
weather is warm, the
eggs may hatch
in a few days.

The Eggs Hatch

The caterpillars eat their way out of the tops of their eggs. They do not look at all like their parents. They have eight pairs of legs, no wings, and large jaws for eating leaves.

Some types, such as the peacock caterpillars, live together in a group. They move to the top of the plant, where they spin a nest of silk. This will help protect the caterpillars from bad weather and enemies.

Growing Up

The hungry caterpillars eat
almost nonstop. Once they
have munched through one
leaf, they move on to the next.
The caterpillars grow very quickly.
They must shed their old skin
when they grow too big
for it. The caterpillars
have a new skin
underneath.

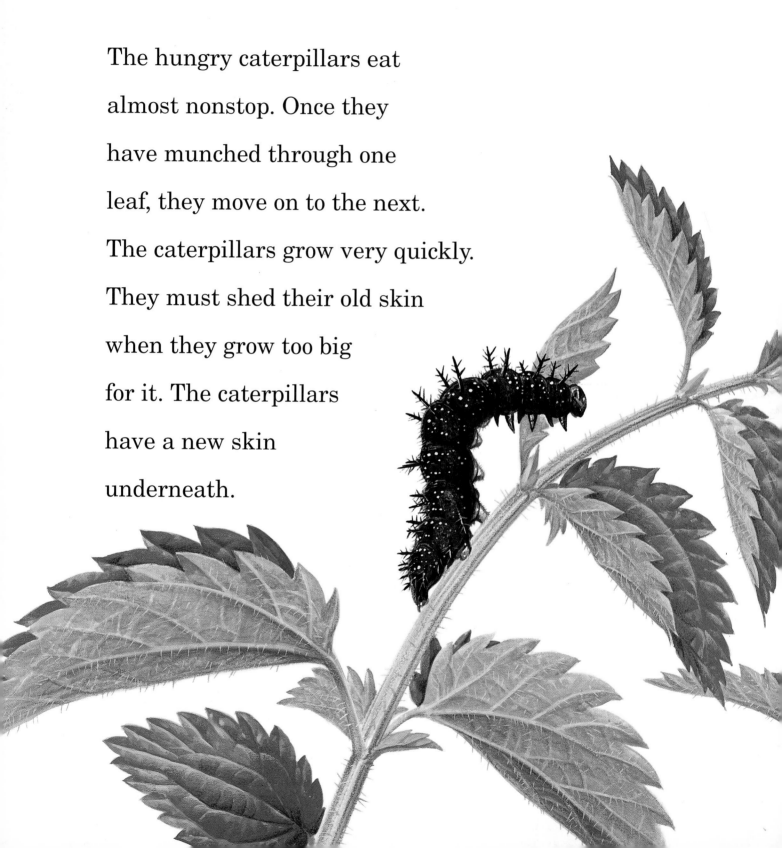

When a caterpillar has shed its skin several times, it is fully grown. It crawls away on its own to find a safe place. Then, the caterpillar sheds its skin for the last time and becomes a pupa enclosed in a chrysalis.

The Chrysalis

You may see a chrysalis
hanging upside down
and sticking to a plant
with a blob of silk.
Inside the chrysalis
the caterpillar begins
to change shape. This is
called metamorphosis.

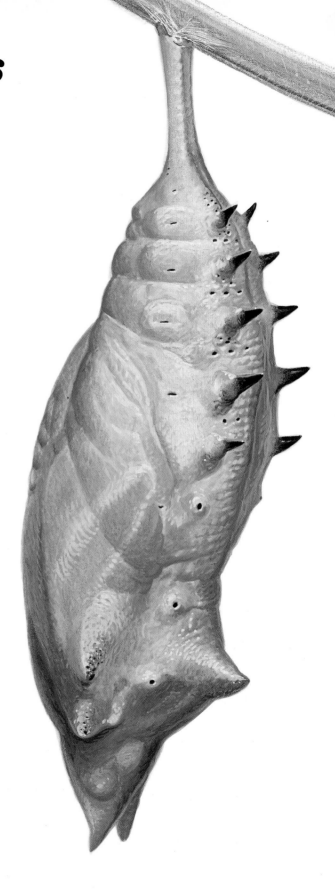

A chrysalis cannot move,
except for an occasional wiggle.
It is in danger of being
eaten by other animals. This is
why a chrysalis is green—other
animals will have trouble finding it.
You must never touch a chrysalis
because it is very delicate.

19

A New Butterfly

After about two weeks, the chrysalis
splits open. The caterpillar has
become a beautiful butterfly.
The butterfly crawls out of the
chrysalis. First come the head
and legs and then the body.
The new butterfly is wet, so
it crawls up onto the
empty chrysalis
to dry.

The butterfly's soft wings are crumpled, so it cannot fly yet. The butterfly pumps blood into its wings and very slowly they become their full size. After one hour, the butterfly is ready to fly for the first time.

Feeding

The new butterflies
flutter from plant to plant
looking for food. They no
longer have jaws for eating
leaves. Butterflies have a special
long tongue for sucking up a flower's
nectar. You may see butterflies on buddleia
and other plants. A butterfly's tongue is rolled up
out of the way when it is not feeding.

22

On a hot day, you may see butterflies drinking from a puddle or pond. In the autumn, some butterflies also feed on rotting fruit. Those types that hibernate must feed on lots of sweet food to last them through the winter when they are asleep.

Escaping from Danger

Butterflies are often eaten by birds. The peacock butterfly has patterns on its wings that look like eyes. If a bird comes too close, the butterfly opens and closes its wings. This makes a hissing sound. The eye patterns look like the eyes of a hungry owl, and they frighten birds away.

The underside of the butterfly's wings are dark. When its wings are closed it looks like a dead leaf. These dark markings are also good for hiding on tree bark.

Helping Butterflies

As we build new roads and our towns become bigger, the countryside is getting smaller. The flowers that the butterflies feed on are disappearing. So are the plants that caterpillars eat.

You can help butterflies by growing the right plants in your yard. Plant plenty of flowering plants on which the butterflies can feed. You could even grow some plants for caterpillars to eat. If you have only a small yard, you could grow flowers in a planter or a window box.

Other Butterflies and Their Caterpillars

Here are some other butterflies you might see.

The red admiral is a brightly colored butterfly seen in gardens and in the countryside.

You may see the
orange-tip butterfly in a
country lane or in
a backyard.

Some people think the large white butterfly
is a pest because its caterpillars
like to eat cabbage.

Life of a Butterfly

1 What is a butterfly?

2 Hibernation

3 Mating

4 The eggs

5 The eggs hatch

6 Growing up

7 The chrysalis

8 A new butterfly

9 Feeding

10 Escaping from danger

11 Helping butterflies

Glossary

caterpillar The wormlike larvae that hatch from the eggs of butterflies and moths.

chrysalis Shell-like covering of pupa stage of butterfly development. Inside the hard chrysalis, the whole body changes, with the wings, legs, and body of the adult insect developing.

hibernate To pass the winter in a sleepy condition, without eating or moving.

insects Small creatures that have a body divided into head, thorax, and abdomen, three pairs of legs, and (in most species) two pairs of wings.

larva The first stage of an insect.

metamorphosis The rapid change from a larva into an adult, as in the change from chrysalis to butterfly or from tadpole to frog.

pupa The form of a butterfly or moth while it is in the chrysalis.

Index